BIBLE

Memory Plan

BIBLE

Memory Plan

Pamela L. McQuade

BARBOUR
PUBLISHING

Published by Barbour Publishing, Inc., P.O. Box 719, Uhrichsville, Ohio 44683, www.barbourbooks.com

Our mission is to publish and distribute inspirational products offering exceptional value and biblical encouragement to the masses.

Member of the
Evangelical Christian
Publishers Association

Printed in the United States of America.

Introduction

The *Bible Memory Plan* is designed for anyone who wants to memorize the Bible. Fazed by that thought, because you aren't "good at memorizing"? Then this is just the book for you. The plan starts out with short verses and slowly expands to longer passages. Along the way are many tips, including memorization methods and bits of encouragement that make learning easier. Verses are identified by topic, so you can relate them to one another.

To help you keep past verses clear, each week of the plan provides a review section. Once a month, the review section expands to five or six verses. As you go on, feel free to review former memory verses as often as necessary to keep them fresh in your mind.

Already have one of these verses memorized? Go to More Verses to Memorize at the end of the book and choose a verse that isn't already in your mind. Otherwise, this list can be used to continue memorization once you've completed the fifty-two verses here.

WEEK 1

BIBLE MEMORY VERSE

*In the beginning God created
the heaven and the earth.*
GENESIS 1:1 KJV

*In the beginning God created
the heavens and the earth.*
GENESIS 1:1 NIV

*In the beginning God created
the heavens and the earth.*
GENESIS 1:1 NLT

Topic

Our God

Insight

These opening words of the Old Testament form the foundation of our knowledge of God.

Tips and Encouragement

- Each week's scripture is quoted from three Bible versions. Memorize the one that is most familiar to you or that you will be most comfortable using in daily life.

- Read the verse aloud to yourself or whomever you're memorizing with. On the first day or two, your goal will be to get a feel for the whole verse. Every other day focus on memorizing a few words at a time.

- If you are single, you may want to memorize with a friend or fellow church member.

- Write out the verse on an index card and use it throughout the day to review the verse. Before you start memorizing, check what you've written against the text to make sure you copied it correctly.

- Some people learn better by sound, while others learn visually. Identify how you learn best and spend most of your time using that kind of method. Later chapters will introduce you to many methods of memorization.

- After you finish your week of memorization, keep one copy of an index card with your memory verse, so you can use it to review the verse in following weeks. Make sure you write the topic on the top of the card, so you can review verses by topic if you want to.

WEEK 2

BIBLE MEMORY VERSE

*I can do all things through Christ
which strengtheneth me.*
PHILIPPIANS 4:13 KJV

*I can do all this through him
who gives me strength.*
PHILIPPIANS 4:13 NIV

*For I can do everything through Christ,
who gives me strength.*
PHILIPPIANS 4:13 NLT

Topic

Christian Life

Insight

Whether Paul had much or lacked much, he told the Philippian church he had learned to be content. The apostle trusted in God's strength, not his own.

Tips and Encouragement

- Choose a calm part of the day to focus on your Bible memorization. The fewer interruptions you have, the more likely you are to be successful.

- Establish a set time when you will memorize the verse every day. Spend that time focusing on the verse and its meaning. Then review the verse over and over again then or through-out the day when you have a few minutes.

- Don't forget to memorize the book, chapter, and verse. It is irritating to have trouble finding a verse just because you forgot to memorize where it's located. And if you are witnessing to someone, they are more likely to believe your testimony if you really know where the verses are.

■ It's best to choose one version of the Bible for your memorization, because changing versions can become confusing. But if you do use more than one version, be sure to memorize the version along with the book, chapter, and verse.

REVIEW

Genesis 1:1

WEEK 3

BIBLE MEMORY VERSE

Thy word is a lamp unto my feet,
and a light unto my path.
PSALM 119:105 KJV

Your word is a lamp for my feet,
a light on my path.
PSALM 119:105 NIV

Your word is a lamp to guide my feet
and a light for my path.
PSALM 119:105 NLT

TOPIC

God's Word

INSIGHT

Psalm 119, the longest chapter in the Bible, is all about God's Word. This verse tells us that God's Word guides our lives. If God thinks His Word is important for believers, how should we respond to it?

TIPS AND ENCOURAGEMENT

≡ When a verse paints a picture, as this one does, use its images to help you remember it. Visual images of a lamp, feet, a light, and a path can remind you of key parts of the verse.

≡ Don't just focus on each word when you are memorizing. Consider the meaning of the whole verse, and it will be easier to memorize.

- Be encouraged as you begin to remember portions of your verse. If you get a few words wrong, do not worry. Look at your accomplishments and continue to work on the verse.

- Sometimes a verse may provide encouragement for a situation you are in. Allow this element of God's truth to fill your soul.

- Finish your verse in less than a week? Go back and review the ones you've already memorized. Make it a habit to keep reviewing what you've already done. When you have many verses memorized, it will be a good habit to have developed.

REVIEW

Genesis 1:1
Philippians 4:13

WEEK 4

BIBLE MEMORY VERSE

God is my strength and power:
and he maketh my way perfect.
2 SAMUEL 22:33 KJV

It is God who arms me with strength
and keeps my way secure.
2 SAMUEL 22:33 NIV

God is my strong fortress,
and he makes my way perfect.
2 SAMUEL 22:33 NLT

TOPIC

Our God

INSIGHT

David spoke these words of praise after God delivered him from all his enemies. How is He our strong fortress?

TIPS AND ENCOURAGEMENT

≡ In order to memorize effectively, you'll need to commit time to it. No one else can do this for you — it is your choice. But what is more important than your relationship with God? Because you love Him, make the time to memorize His Word.

≡ While you are memorizing, ask yourself what each verse means and how it relates to your Christian life. You are not memorizing just to have words in your head but to make them part of your faith walk.

≡ If you make mistakes, go back and reread your text aloud. As you repeatedly reread the whole text, you will begin to memorize it unknowingly. At some point, you will look at the text and realize that you have it almost down pat. This is the point at which you want to fine-tune your memorization. Look for words you have trouble remembering and begin to focus on them.

REVIEW

Genesis 1:1
Philippians 4:13
Psalm 119:105

WEEK 5

BIBLE MEMORY VERSE

So then faith cometh by hearing,
and hearing by the word of God.
ROMANS 10:17 KJV

Consequently, faith comes from hearing
the message, and the message is heard
through the word about Christ.
ROMANS 10:17 NIV

So faith comes from hearing, that is,
hearing the Good News about Christ.
ROMANS 10:17 NLT

Topic

Faith

Insight

People believe because they've heard the gospel message. How can those who have never heard know Christ? What will help them hear?

Tips and Encouragement

- Avoid the temptation to memorize too much too soon. You will have a sense of accomplishment when you get some verses in your head in a short time. If you rush it you may become discouraged and not want to continue.

- If one week contains a verse you have already memorized, replace it with one from the More Verses to Memorize section at the end of the book.

- When you have most of your verse down pat, continue to compare it to the original, in case your memorization is not quite accurate.

- Remind yourself that knowing the Bible well is important to your Christian life. Sharing your faith and encouraging others requires that you have God's Word in your mind.

REVIEW

Genesis 1:1
Philippians 4:13
Psalm 119:105
2 Samuel 22:33

WEEK 6

BIBLE MEMORY VERSE

*A soft answer turneth away wrath:
but grievous words stir up anger.*
PROVERBS 15:1 KJV

*A gentle answer turns away wrath,
but a harsh word stirs up anger.*
PROVERBS 15:1 NIV

*A gentle answer deflects anger,
but harsh words make tempers flare.*
PROVERBS 15:1 NLT

Topic

Christian Life

Insight

The book of Proverbs offers practical advice on how to live for God. How can we benefit from it?

Tips and Encouragement

- Absolutely can't find time to memorize a new verse today? Use your limited time to review the verses you've already memorized. But work on the new verse tomorrow.

- Forgetting to carry your memorization card with you? Make sure you have one in your car, wallet, and at work (so you can study it on lunchtime or break time).

- If you've memorized all the verses so far, be encouraged. At the end of this week, you'll have six verses memorized and have proved to yourself that you have the commitment to memorize the Word.

REVIEW

Now that you have five verses under your belt, review them all.

Genesis 1:1
Philippians 4:13
Psalm 119:105
2 Samuel 22:33
Romans 10:17

WEEK 7

BIBLE MEMORY VERSE

*Every word of God is pure: he is a shield
unto them that put their trust in him.*
PROVERBS 30:5 KJV

*"Every word of God is flawless; he is a shield
to those who take refuge in him."*
PROVERBS 30:5 NIV

*Every word of God proves true. He is a shield
to all who come to him for protection.*
PROVERBS 30:5 NLT

Topic

God's Word

Insight

Agur the son of Jakeh, who penned this verse, recognized how small his store of wisdom was, compared to God's. He encouraged others to trust in the Lord's every word.

Tips and Encouragement

≡ Spend a lot of time on your home computer? If you use the Windows program, you can type your verse into the Marquee screensaver. Read your verse before you move your mouse.

≡ Rewrite your verse every day. Leave copies where you can read them often.

≡ Constantly carry one copy of your verse with you. Review it in the doctor's office, as you wait for a friend, or as you take public transportation.

≡ If you'd like to memorize verses more quickly, you can memorize two verses in a week. When you have finished memorizing the verses here, pick up on the More Verses to Memorize in the back of the book.

REVIEW

Psalm 119:105
2 Samuel 22:33
Romans 10:17
Proverbs 15:1

WEEK 8

BIBLE MEMORY VERSE

*A new commandment I give unto you,
that ye love one another; as I have loved you,
that ye also love one another.*
JOHN 13:34 KJV

*A new command I give you: Love one another.
As I have loved you, so you must love one another.*
JOHN 13:34 NIV

*So now I am giving you a new commandment:
Love each other. Just as I have loved you,
you should love each other.*
JOHN 13:34 NLT

Topic

Christian Life

Insight

At the Passover supper Jesus gave this command to His disciples. Following His death, they would need His love as their cohesive force.

Tips and Encouragement

≡ Look at the structure of longer verses, which may include parts such as an introduction, main concept, secondary ideas, or conclusion. (Each verse may have all of these or just a few of them.)

≡ Once you've identified the parts of the verse, aim at learning one portion at a time. Focus on the first section of the verse, perhaps up to the first punctuation mark, and memorize six to ten words at a time. Breaking the verse into sections helps you see that the whole verse is made up of easily memorized pieces. Take these pieces and work on them one by one. Read through the whole verse periodically as you are memorizing each portion.

≡ When you have the first section under your belt, you are ready to focus on another. Continue in this manner, memorizing a few more words each day and reviewing the old ones, until you have the whole verse memorized.

≡ When you have memorized each portion of the verse, go over the whole verse, to fix the whole thing in your mind. Focus on any areas you have trouble remembering, and fine-tune those spots.

≡ Speaking to the *Boston Globe*, actress Elizabeth Aspenlieder described how she memorizes her parts:

"It's almost like creating a quilt. I learn a piece, and then I go back over the piece I've just learned and add to it, and then I add another piece, and then I kind of do the stitches around the pieces I've just learned."

REVIEW

2 Samuel 22:33
Romans 10:17
Proverbs 15:1
Proverbs 30:5

WEEK 9

BIBLE MEMORY VERSE

If we confess our sins, he is faithful and just to forgive us our sins, and to cleanse us from all unrighteousness.
1 JOHN 1:9 KJV

If we confess our sins, he is faithful and just and will forgive us our sins and purify us from all unrighteousness.
1 JOHN 1:9 NIV

But if we confess our sins to him, he is faithful and just to forgive us our sins and to cleanse us from all wickedness.
1 JOHN 1:9 NLT

TOPIC

Salvation

INSIGHT

God is perfect, and sin separates us from Him. John describes confession's role in our relationship with Him.

TIPS AND ENCOURAGEMENT

≡ Having trouble keeping up with your memorization? Review the memorization tips from earlier chapters. Increasingly focus on the most successful methods as you learn longer verses.

≡ Remind yourself that memorizing scripture not only helps you share your faith, it also brings you encouragement. God can bring His Word to your mind when doubt seeks to slip in, but only if you already have that Word there.

- If you find a verse you'd like to memorize, add it to the list of More Verses to Memorize in the back of the book, and work on it when you have finished these. Memorizing the Bible is not a rush job, but a lifelong commitment.

REVIEW

Romans 10:17
Proverbs 15:1
Proverbs 30:5
John 13:34

WEEK 10

BIBLE MEMORY VERSE

*For by grace are ye saved through faith;
and that not of yourselves: It is the gift of God:
Not of works, lest any man should boast.*
EPHESIANS 2:8–9 KJV

*For it is by grace you have been saved,
through faith – and this is not from yourselves,
it is the gift of God – not by works,
so that no one can boast.*
EPHESIANS 2:8–9 NIV

*God saved you by his grace when you believed.
And you can't take credit for this; it is a gift from
God. Salvation is not a reward for the good things
we have done, so none of us can boast about it.*
EPHESIANS 2:8–9 NLT

TOPIC

Salvation

INSIGHT

The apostle Paul describes God's gracious salvation, in which He took sinful humans and gave them new life in Him. We could never earn this great gift from our Lord.

TIPS AND ENCOURAGEMENT

- Do not be intimidated by having to memorize two verses at a time. Start by reading the whole passage. Then continue in the way you began, breaking each verse down into smaller passages to memorize.

- If your verse has been put to music, sing it. Download music to listen to whenever you can, or use a CD. But be certain the musician has not taken artistic license with the verse, or you may not be memorizing the verse accurately.

- Or make up your own tune for your verse. It does not have to be an award-winning ditty, just something that helps you remember the words. Hum it to yourself throughout the day!

- Having trouble with your memorization commitment? Ask yourself why you are memorizing. If it's because you want to impress others, God cannot bless your time with His Word. Focus on the real importance of knowing God's Word by carefully reading Psalm 119. Why does God say it's important to know what He's said?

REVIEW

Proverbs 15:1
Proverbs 30:5
John 13:34
1 John 1:9

WEEK 11

BIBLE MEMORY VERSE

Beloved, let us love one another: for love is of God; and every one that loveth is born of God, and knoweth God.
1 JOHN 4:7 KJV

Dear friends, let us love one another, for love comes from God. Everyone who loves has been born of God and knows God.
1 JOHN 4:7 NIV

Dear friends, let us continue to love one another, for love comes from God. Anyone who loves is a child of God and knows God.
1 JOHN 4:7 NLT

Topic

Christian Life

Insight

Love for God and others is a key part of the Christian life. John points out that we can be known as Christians by our love for one another.

Tips and Encouragement

- Try to memorize at a time of day when your mind is alert. If you are tired when you try to memorize, you may find you don't remember much.

- Need more tips or encouragement? Read ahead in that section of the *Bible Memory Plan*.

- Forgetting the verses you previously memorized? Daily write them down on cards again and review them. Make certain you are using the same version you first memorized, so you do not become confused.

REVIEW

Proverbs 30:5
John 13:34
1 John 1:9
Ephesians 2:8–9

WEEK 12

BIBLE MEMORY VERSE

Many are the afflictions of the righteous:
but the LORD delivereth him out of them all.
PSALM 34:19 KJV

The righteous person may have many troubles,
but the LORD delivers him from them all.
PSALM 34:19 NIV

The righteous person faces many troubles,
but the LORD comes to the rescue each time.
PSALM 34:19 NLT

TOPIC

Our God

INSIGHT

When David wrote this psalm he was in
the midst of trouble, having been driven
out from the protection of the king of Gath.
David must have feared that his enemy,
King Saul, would destroy him, yet he spoke
this praise.

TIPS AND ENCOURAGEMENT

≡ Commit to and protect your memorization time. You may need to change
when you do it, but don't let the
world's cares force you to set it aside.

≡ When you've partly memorized
a verse, write out the entire verse
and underline any words you are
struggling with, then focus on those
words.

- To encourage yourself, give yourself periodic rewards for accomplishing your memorization goals. When you finish this week, give yourself a three-month reward — go to a special coffee shop or have lunch with a friend. Or buy yourself something that you've always wanted.

REVIEW

Proverbs 15:1
Proverbs 30:5
John 13:34
1 John 1:9
Ephesians 2:8–9
1 John 4:7

WEEK 13

BIBLE MEMORY VERSE

Call unto me, and I will answer thee,
and show thee great and mighty things,
which thou knowest not.
JEREMIAH 33:3 KJV

"Call to me and I will answer you and tell you
great and unsearchable things you do not know."
JEREMIAH 33:3 NIV

"Ask me and I will tell you remarkable secrets
you do not know about things to come."
JEREMIAH 33:3 NLT

TOPIC

Our God

INSIGHT

When Jeremiah was shut up in prison, God gave this promise to him. What great things has God shown you in your Christian life?

TIPS AND ENCOURAGEMENT

≡ When you are reviewing a verse from memory, try to "see" it as you have written it down and read it from that written version.

≡ Think about times when your memorization helped you. Have you spoken to someone about Christ and had the words in your mind? Have you thought of a verse and known that God is working in your own life?

≡ As you are memorizing, study these verses, too. Read the context of the verse to find out what is happening. Use a Bible dictionary, commentary, or other study aids to find out more about the passage.

- If you do not have many Bible study tools, seek out some online sites that have them available. You may even want to print out some passages, to help your study. Just be certain any commentaries you study are on target theologically.

REVIEW

1 John 1:9
Ephesians 2:8–9
1 John 4:7
Psalm 34:19

WEEK 14

BIBLE MEMORY VERSE

The fear of the LORD is the beginning of knowledge:
but fools despise wisdom and instruction.
PROVERBS 1:7 KJV

The fear of the LORD is the beginning of knowledge,
but fools despise wisdom and instruction.
PROVERBS 1:7 NIV

Fear of the LORD is the foundation of true knowledge,
but fools despise wisdom and discipline.
PROVERBS 1:7 NLT

TOPIC

Seeking God

INSIGHT

Those who do not fear God will never share in His wisdom. Do not be surprised when others despise Him and your faith.

TIPS AND ENCOURAGEMENT

≡ If others do not support you in your memorization, be kind to them. Learning the scriptures but offending others is not a good Christian testimony. Work to balance compassion and your commitment to God's Word.

≡ If your spouse won't memorize with you, prayerfully invite another family member to do so.

≡ Not a morning person? Maybe you need to memorize in the evening. Everyone's body clock is different. Make the best use of yours.

Review

1 John 1:9
Ephesians 2:8–9
1 John 4:7
Psalm 34:19
Jeremiah 33:3

WEEK 15

BIBLE MEMORY VERSE

There is therefore now no condemnation to them which are in Christ Jesus, who walk not after the flesh, but after the Spirit.
ROMANS 8:1 KJV

Therefore, there is now no condemnation for those who are in Christ Jesus.
ROMANS 8:1 NIV

So now there is no condemnation for those who belong to Christ Jesus.
ROMANS 8:1 NLT

Topic

Salvation

Insight

Though all these versions focus on the salvation Jesus brings to believers, the King James Version follows a later manuscript that adds the last part of the verse.

Tips and Encouragement

≡ Scripture translations may vary slightly, based on the original-language manuscript that was used. Modern translations are more likely to use an earlier manuscript than older translations, like the King James Version. But they often note variations in other manuscripts, as the New International Version does for this verse.

- If you are memorizing without referring to your written text and begin to become confused, stop! Wait until you have your text with you, so you do not have to correct a wrong memorization.

REVIEW

1 John 4:7
Psalm 34:19
Jeremiah 33:3
Proverbs 1:7

WEEK 16

BIBLE MEMORY VERSE

For I am not ashamed of the gospel of Christ:
for it is the power of God unto salvation to every
one that believeth; to the Jew first,
and also to the Greek.
ROMANS 1:16 KJV

For I am not ashamed of the gospel,
because it is the power of God that brings
salvation to everyone who believes:
first to the Jew, then to the Gentile.
ROMANS 1:16 NIV

For I am not ashamed of this Good News
about Christ. It is the power of God at work,
saving everyone who believes—
the Jew first and also the Gentile.
ROMANS 1:16 NLT

Topic

Salvation

Insight

God can work in the lives of those who hear the Good News. Scripture is designed to save souls, no matter what background those people come from.

Tips and Encouragement

≡ Are you feeling a bit bored with your favorite way of memorizing? Shake yourself up by doing something different: plaster your verse on the bathroom mirror or sing it in the shower while you prepare for your day. Try some other methods in the Tips and Encouragement sections that you haven't used before.

≡ Keep working on your quilt of Bible memorization. Are you making a wall hanging or a real cover for the cold days in your life? You are the one who decides how much of the Word you will put in your mind.

REVIEW

Psalm 34:19
Jeremiah 33:3
Proverbs 1:7
Romans 8:1

WEEK 17

BIBLE MEMORY VERSE

But the fruit of the Spirit is love, joy, peace, long-suffering, gentleness, goodness, faith, meekness, temperance: against such there is no law.
GALATIANS 5:22–23 KJV

But the fruit of the Spirit is love, joy, peace, forbearance, kindness, goodness, faithfulness, gentleness and self-control. Against such things there is no law.
GALATIANS 5:22–23 NIV

But the Holy Spirit produces this kind of fruit in our lives: love, joy, peace, patience, kindness, goodness, faithfulness, gentleness, and self-control. There is no law against these things!
GALATIANS 5:22–23 NLT

Topic

Christian Life

Insight

Paul pictures believers as bearing the fruit of good works and attitudes in their lives. This is living by the Spirit.

Tips and Encouragement

≡ Make use of the verse you are learn-ing by sharing it with someone else. Quote it, then tell them what it means or how it has affected your life.

≡ Are you memorizing only a couple of days a week? Recommit yourself to daily memorization by identifying why you aren't being committed and changing whatever gets in the way.

≡ Remind yourself of the benefits of knowing the Word well.

Review

Jeremiah 33:3
Proverbs 1:7
Romans 8:1
Romans 1:16

WEEK 18

BIBLE MEMORY VERSE

For the preaching of the cross is to them that perish foolishness; but unto us which are saved it is the power of God.
1 CORINTHIANS 1:18 KJV

For the message of the cross is foolishness to those who are perishing, but to us who are being saved it is the power of God.
1 CORINTHIANS 1:18 NIV

The message of the cross is foolish to those who are headed for destruction! But we who are being saved know it is the very power of God.
1 CORINTHIANS 1:18 NLT

Topic

Salvation

Insight

The cross seems foolish to unbelievers but is the very center of the faith to those who believe. God's wisdom is way beyond the wisdom of man.

Tips and Encouragement

≡ When reviewing verses, put more than one on a file card to carry with you. Use the back of the card, too. That way you won't have a large stack of cards to carry. You can group your verses by topic.

Review

Psalm 34:19
Jeremiah 33:3
Proverbs 1:7
Romans 8:1
Romans 1:16
Galatians 5:22–23

WEEK 19

Bible Memory Verse

In the beginning was the Word,
and the Word was with God, and the Word was
God. The same was in the beginning with God.
JOHN 1:1–2 KJV

In the beginning was the Word,
and the Word was with God, and the Word was
God. He was with God in the beginning.
JOHN 1:1–2 NIV

In the beginning the Word already existed.
The Word was with God, and the Word was God.
He existed in the beginning with God.
JOHN 1:1–2 NLT

Topic

Our God

Insight

Who is this mysterious Word? It's Jesus
(see John 1:14). It's no coincidence that these
verses parallel the beginning of Genesis.
John is declaring that Jesus is God, and Lord
of creation.

Tips and Encouragement

- Sometimes review your verses
  according to topic instead of in
  the order you've memorized them
  in. Organize your verses by topic,
  and review each group separately.
  This will make review time more
  interesting and will also give you a
  firmer grasp on what scripture says
  about these subjects.

- If a verse seems confusing to you,
  pick up your Bible and read a few
  verses around it or even the whole
  chapter. John 1 is an amazing descrip-
  tion of Jesus that appears nowhere
  else in scripture.

REVIEW

Romans 8:1
Romans 1:16
Galatians 5:22–23
1 Corinthians 1:18

WEEK 20

BIBLE MEMORY VERSE

Trust in the LORD with all thine heart;
and lean not unto thine own understanding.
In all thy ways acknowledge him,
and he shall direct thy paths.
PROVERBS 3:5–6 KJV

Trust in the LORD with all your heart
and lean not on your own understanding;
in all your ways submit to him, and he
will make your paths straight.
PROVERBS 3:5–6 NIV

Trust in the LORD with all your heart;
do not depend on your own understanding.
Seek his will in all you do, and he will
show you which path to take.
PROVERBS 3:5–6 NLT

TOPIC

Faith

INSIGHT

When wise King Solomon gave advice to his son, he encouraged him to trust in God, not his own wisdom. Even the most astute human cannot direct a life as well as God can.

TIPS AND ENCOURAGEMENT

≡ What do you know about the people who penned or are involved in the verses you are memorizing? If you know that God gave King Solomon great wisdom, but the wise king advised others to rely on God, this passage has a lot more meaning.

≡ If you aren't studying the Bible, use these verses to start a study. Find out as much as you can about each verse. Do you need to look up some you've already studied?

REVIEW

Romans 1:16
Galatians 5:22–23
1 Corinthians 1:18
John 1:1–2

WEEK 21

BIBLE MEMORY VERSE

Know ye not that ye are the temple of God,
and that the Spirit of God dwelleth in you?
1 CORINTHIANS 3:16 KJV

Don't you know that you yourselves
are God's temple and that God's Spirit
dwells in your midst?
1 CORINTHIANS 3:16 NIV

Don't you realize that all of you together
are the temple of God and that the
Spirit of God lives in you?
1 CORINTHIANS 3:16 NLT

TOPIC

Christian Life

INSIGHT

Now that there is no earthly temple building, God has made His people His temple, filling them with His Spirit.

TIPS AND ENCOURAGEMENT

- When starting to work on a verse, ask yourself questions such as: What does this verse mean to me in my Christian life? How would the world be different if this were not true? How can this help me in my Christian life?

- When you memorize, you are deepening your knowledge of God. Don't let your focus be only on memorization success but on how you are building your relationship with your Lord.

REVIEW

Galatians 5:22–23
1 Corinthians 1:18
John 1:1–2
Proverbs 3:5–6

WEEK 22

BIBLE MEMORY VERSE

*I will lift up mine eyes unto the hills,
from whence cometh my help. My help cometh
from the LORD, which made heaven and earth.*
PSALM 121:1–2 KJV

*I lift up my eyes to the mountains –
where does my help come from?
My help comes from the LORD,
the Maker of heaven and earth.*
PSALM 121:1–2 NIV

*I look up to the mountains – does my help come
from there? My help comes from the LORD,
who made heaven and earth!*
PSALM 121:1–2 NLT

Topic

Our God

Insight

The psalmist glorifies the Lord, who helps and protects His people. Who else can we trust this way?

Tips and Encouragement

- Even though you are not memorizing all three versions, read over the translations from the other Bible versions. What insight can you get from the way another translator sees this verse?

- What does this verse teach you about the topic? What other verses have you memorized on this topic? How do they relate to each other?

- Remember to add to the quilt of your Bible memorization each day, piece by piece. Soon you will have a warm blanket that will protect you from the evil one's darts.

REVIEW

1 Corinthians 1:18
John 1:1–2
Proverbs 3:5–6
1 Corinthians 3:16

WEEK 23

BIBLE MEMORY VERSE

*But without faith it is impossible to please him:
for he that cometh to God must believe that he is,
and that he is a rewarder of them that
diligently seek him.*
HEBREWS 11:6 KJV

*And without faith it is impossible to please God,
because anyone who comes to him must believe
that he exists and that he rewards those
who earnestly seek him.*
HEBREWS 11:6 NIV

*And it is impossible to please God without faith.
Anyone who wants to come to him must believe
that God exists and that he rewards those
who sincerely seek him.*
HEBREWS 11:6 NLT

TOPIC

Faith

INSIGHT

This is a portion of the impressive faith chapter of Hebrews, which describes the importance of faith, focusing on the actions of Old Testament believers.

TIPS AND ENCOURAGEMENT

- How can you use this verse in your personal life? When you share your faith with other Christians? When you witness?

- What are the best times in your day for memorization? Are you making the most of them? If you can't memorize at your usual time, are you able to find another patch in your day when you can do it? Be persistent in your memorization.

REVIEW

John 1:1–2
Proverbs 3:5–6
1 Corinthians 3:16
Psalm 121:1–2

WEEK 24

BIBLE MEMORY VERSE

*And we know that all things work together for
good to them that love God, to them who are the
called according to his purpose.*
ROMANS 8:28 KJV

*And we know that in all things God works for the
good of those who love him, who have been called
according to his purpose.*
ROMANS 8:28 NIV

*And we know that God causes everything to work
together for the good of those who love God and
are called according to his purpose for them.*
ROMANS 8:28 NLT

TOPIC

Our God

INSIGHT

In Romans 8 Paul encourages us to look forward to our future in Christ as the Spirit works in our lives.

TIPS AND ENCOURAGEMENT

≡ What insights have you gotten about God by memorizing His Word? How is it different from simply reading the Word?

≡ Memorization can strengthen you by preparing you for whatever you face in your Christian life. Can you answer the questions of seekers more readily, find encouragement, and withstand temptation when it comes?

REVIEW

1 Corinthians 1:18
John 1:1–2
Proverbs 3:5–6
1 Corinthians 3:16
Psalm 121:1–2
Hebrews 11:6

WEEK 25

BIBLE MEMORY VERSE

*Wherefore, my beloved brethren, let every man
be swift to hear, slow to speak, slow to wrath:
For the wrath of man worketh not the
righteousness of God.*
JAMES 1:19–20 KJV

*My dear brothers and sisters, take note of this:
Everyone should be quick to listen,
slow to speak and slow to become angry,
because human anger does not produce
the righteousness that God desires.*
JAMES 1:19–20 NIV

*Understand this, my dear brothers and sisters:
You must all be quick to listen, slow to speak,
and slow to get angry. Human anger does not
produce the righteousness God desires.*
JAMES 1:19–20 NLT

Topic

Christian Life

Insight

The book of James is rich in wisdom for living the Christian life, including this advice on avoiding anger.

Tips and Encouragement

≡ Some portions of the Bible provide highly practical advice on how to live as a Christian. Be encouraged that God provides much information on how to live for Him and with others. Use it!

≡ When you're reviewing verses, don't always take them in the same order. This unexpectedness will help you memorize them more effectively.

REVIEW

1 Corinthians 3:16
Psalm 121:1–2
Hebrews 11:6
Romans 8:28

WEEK 26

BIBLE MEMORY VERSE

*Finally, my brethren, be strong in the Lord,
and in the power of his might. Put on the whole
armour of God, that ye may be able to stand
against the wiles of the devil.*
EPHESIANS 6:10–11 KJV

*Finally, be strong in the Lord and in his mighty
power. Put on the full armor of God, so that you
can take your stand against the devil's schemes.*
EPHESIANS 6:10–11 NIV

*A final word: Be strong in the Lord and in his
mighty power. Put on all of God's armor so that
you will be able to stand firm against all
strategies of the devil.*
EPHESIANS 6:10–11 NLT

Topic

Christian Life

Insight

Paul shows believers that their strength is not in their ability to obey God, but in their Lord's power. Putting on God's armor protects the faithful from all of Satan's wiles. In the following verses, the apostle describes this armor that helps Christians stand strong in the faith.

Tips and Encouragement

- Don't forget to carry your scripture cards with you, wherever you go. Going on vacation? Pack them so you can review them on the plane or during a long drive.

- Remember a time when God has reminded you of a scripture you memorized just at the moment when you needed it. Aren't you glad you memorized that verse?

- Congratulations. You are halfway through a year of memorization, if you have kept up with the whole Bible Memory Plan. If it's taken you more than half of a year, you may not have been speedy, but you were faithful.

REVIEW

Psalm 121:1–2
Hebrews 11:6
Romans 8:28
James 1:19–20

WEEK 27

BIBLE MEMORY VERSE

Humble yourselves therefore under the mighty hand of God, that he may exalt you in due time: Casting all your care upon him; for he careth for you.
1 PETER 5:6–7 KJV

Humble yourselves, therefore, under God's mighty hand, that he may lift you up in due time. Cast all your anxiety on him because he cares for you.
1 PETER 5:6–7 NIV

So humble yourselves under the mighty power of God, and at the right time he will lift you up in honor. Give all your worries and cares to God, for he cares about you.
1 PETER 5:6–7 NLT

TOPIC

Seeking God

INSIGHT

God is not trying to develop believers' pride. Though we don't like the idea of being humble, it is part of the Christian portfolio. When we are humble, we allow God to control our lives and futures.

TIPS AND ENCOURAGEMENT

≡ How have you been blessed by your memorization? Share this with a Christian friend whom you can encourage to start memorizing, too.

≡ When you first started memorizing, was it hard for you? How has practice made it easier for you?

REVIEW

Hebrews 11:6
Romans 8:28
James 1:19–20
Ephesians 6:10–11

WEEK 28

BIBLE MEMORY VERSE

Who can find a virtuous woman?
For her price is far above rubies.
The heart of her husband doth safely trust in her,
so that he shall have no need of spoil.
PROVERBS 31:10–11 KJV

A wife of noble character who can find?
She is worth far more than rubies.
Her husband has full confidence in
her and lacks nothing of value.
PROVERBS 31:10–11 NIV

Who can find a virtuous and capable wife?
She is more precious than rubies.
Her husband can trust her,
and she will greatly enrich his life.
PROVERBS 31:10–11 NLT

Topic

Christian Life

Insight

King Lemuel's mother gave him this wise
advice on marriage. Many believers have
discovered the wisdom of such a union.

Tips and Encouragement

- Even when you think you have the
  verse well memorized, periodically
  check yourself against the written
  text, until you have it down perfectly.

- Continue repeating a verse, even
  after you have memorized it. Otherwise, it's easy to forget. Try to make
  the verse a part of your everyday life.
  Think of it when you are driving,
  running an errand, or before you fall
  asleep at night.

REVIEW

Romans 8:28
James 1:19–20
Ephesians 6:10–11
1 Peter 5:6–7

WEEK 29

BIBLE MEMORY VERSE

Come now, and let us reason together,
saith the LORD: though your sins be as scarlet,
they shall be as white as snow; though they be red
like crimson, they shall be as wool.
ISAIAH 1:18 KJV

"Come now, let us settle the matter,"
says the LORD. "Though your sins are like scarlet,
they shall be as white as snow; though they are
red as crimson, they shall be like wool."
ISAIAH 1:18 NIV

"Come now, let's settle this," says the LORD.
"Though your sins are like scarlet, I will make
them as white as snow. Though they are red like
crimson, I will make them as white as wool."
ISAIAH 1:18 NLT

TOPIC

Salvation

INSIGHT

Through the prophet Isaiah, God called His people to turn from their sin and obey Him. Only God can cleanse sin until it's snow white.

TIPS AND ENCOURAGEMENT

- When you have memorized verses on salvation, share them lovingly with those who do not know God. Remember, if you use a verse in anger against someone, you are unlikely to win that soul to Christ.

- What other verses about salvation would you like to memorize? Add them to the More Verses to Memorize section at the back of the book.

REVIEW

James 1:19–20
Ephesians 6:10–11
1 Peter 5:6–7
Proverbs 31:10–11

WEEK 30

BIBLE MEMORY VERSE

*If ye then be risen with Christ, seek those things
which are above, where Christ sitteth on the right
hand of God. Set your affection on things above,
not on things on the earth.*
COLOSSIANS 3:1–2 KJV

*Since, then, you have been raised with Christ,
set your hearts on things above, where Christ is,
seated at the right hand of God. Set your minds
on things above, not on earthly things.*
COLOSSIANS 3:1–2 NIV

*Since you have been raised to new life with Christ,
set your sights on the realities of heaven,
where Christ sits in the place of honor at God's
right hand. Think about the things of heaven,
not the things of earth.*
COLOSSIANS 3:1–2 NLT

TOPIC

Seeking God

INSIGHT

Paul encourages Christians to take their new life in Christ seriously and turn aside from worldly ways.

TIPS AND ENCOURAGEMENT

≡ To be certain you know the chapter and verse for your verses, sometimes begin with the chapter and verse; then try to say the verse aloud. That way you'll know you are certain where each verse comes from.

≡ If a verse does not seem critical to your spiritual life today, memorize it for future reference. God gave us the whole Bible for a purpose, and you never know when a verse will be important to you.

REVIEW

Romans 8:28
James 1:19–20
Ephesians 6:10–11
1 Peter 5:6–7
Proverbs 31:10–11
Isaiah 1:18

WEEK 31

BIBLE MEMORY VERSE

*But they that wait upon the LORD shall renew
their strength; they shall mount up with wings
as eagles; they shall run, and not be weary;
and they shall walk, and not faint.*
ISAIAH 40:31 KJV

*But those who hope in the LORD will renew
their strength. They will soar on wings like
eagles; they will run and not grow weary,
they will walk and not be faint.*
ISAIAH 40:31 NIV

*But those who trust in the LORD will find
new strength. They will soar high on wings
like eagles. They will run and not grow weary.
They will walk and not faint.*
ISAIAH 40:31 NLT

TOPIC

Our God

INSIGHT

Isaiah describes how believers who depend on the everlasting, all-powerful God can rely on His strength.

TIPS AND ENCOURAGEMENT

- ≡ Don't stop writing down your memory verse every day. Having trouble remembering the verses you memorized early on? Write them down for a few days, too, until you have them down pat again.

- ≡ Having trouble remembering which verse goes with which reference? Write down all your verses on a file card and cut off the references with a paper cutter. Then match them up again. Or play a game with your family, having everyone draw verses or references from a pile. Lay out the other cards flat on a table, where they all can be seen and take turns matching the verses and references. Whoever first matches the pulled verses correctly wins.

≡ Is memorizing the Word more exciting now than when you started? What have you learned from doing this?

REVIEW

1 Peter 5:6–7
Proverbs 31:10–11
Isaiah 1:18
Colossians 3:1–2

WEEK 32

BIBLE MEMORY VERSE

*Verily, verily, I say unto you, he that heareth
my word, and believeth on him that sent me,
hath everlasting life, and shall not come into
condemnation; but is passed from death unto life.*
JOHN 5:24 KJV

*"Very truly I tell you, whoever hears my word
and believes him who sent me has eternal life
and will not be judged but has crossed over
from death to life."*
JOHN 5:24 NIV

*"I tell you the truth, those who listen to my
message and believe in God who sent me have
eternal life. They will never be condemned for
their sins, but they have already passed
from death into life."*
JOHN 5:24 NLT

TOPIC

Salvation

INSIGHT

Here Jesus describes His role in salvation as He fulfills the Father's will. No one can know God and fail to know His Son.

TIPS AND ENCOURAGEMENT

= How has your spiritual life benefited from memorizing scripture? Are you more confident in your Christian walk? How have you been able to help others because you know the Word?

= Why is God's Word so important to believers and for those who have yet to believe?

= What goals do you need to set for your Bible memorization plan? What would you like to accomplish when you've finished this book?

REVIEW

Proverbs 31:10–11
Isaiah 1:18
Colossians 3:1–2
Isaiah 40:31

WEEK 33

Bible Memory Verse

God is our refuge and strength, a very present help in trouble. Therefore will not we fear, though the earth be removed, and though the mountains be carried into the midst of the sea.
Psalm 46:1–2 kjv

God is our refuge and strength, an ever-present help in trouble. Therefore we will not fear, though the earth give way and the mountains fall into the heart of the sea.
Psalm 46:1–2 niv

God is our refuge and strength, always ready to help in times of trouble. So we will not fear when earthquakes come and the mountains crumble into the sea.
Psalm 46:1–2 nlt

TOPIC

Our God

INSIGHT

The psalmist describes God as our fortress and the one who provides us with refuge from all our troubles.

TIPS AND ENCOURAGEMENT

- Use the word-picture of God as a fortress to help you memorize this verse. How has God been a fortress in your life?

- Are you still using file cards to help memorize your verses? You may want to keep the older cards in a box or other container that you can have them handy when you need to review them.

REVIEW

Isaiah 1:18
Colossians 3:1–2
Isaiah 40:31
John 5:24

WEEK 34

BIBLE MEMORY VERSE

The LORD also will be a refuge for the oppressed, a refuge in times of trouble. And they that know thy name will put their trust in thee: for thou, LORD, hast not forsaken them that seek thee.
PSALM 9:9–10 KJV

The LORD is a refuge for the oppressed, a stronghold in times of trouble. Those who know your name will trust in you, for you, LORD, have never forsaken those who seek you.
PSALM 9:9–10 NIV

The LORD is a shelter for the oppressed, a refuge in times of trouble. Those who know your name trust in you, for you, O LORD, do not abandon those who search for you.
PSALM 9:9–10 NLT

TOPIC

Our God

INSIGHT

As David recounts God's wonderful deeds, he speaks of God's protection of His people and calls believers to worship Him.

TIPS AND ENCOURAGEMENT

= When scripture has numerous verses on the same topic, God's telling us this is an important concept. How is this verse similar to the one you memorized last week? What does each tell you about God?

= Many Bible verses, like this one, are intensely personal. What does it tell you about God's love for you?

REVIEW

Colossians 3:1–2
Isaiah 40:31
John 5:24
Psalm 46:1–2

WEEK 35

BIBLE MEMORY VERSE

*For the word of God is quick, and powerful,
and sharper than any twoedged sword, piercing
even to the dividing asunder of soul and spirit,
and of the joints and marrow, and is a discerner
of the thoughts and intents of the heart.*
HEBREWS 4:12 KJV

*For the word of God is alive and active.
Sharper than any double-edged sword,
it penetrates even to dividing soul and spirit,
joints and marrow; it judges the thoughts
and attitudes of the heart.*
HEBREWS 4:12 NIV

*For the word of God is alive and powerful.
It is sharper than the sharpest two-edged sword,
cutting between soul and spirit, between joint
and marrow. It exposes our innermost
thoughts and desires.*
HEBREWS 4:12 NLT

TOPIC

God's Word

INSIGHT

God's Word convicts people of their sin and
shows them how their lives cannot live up to
His commandments. Even those who have
come to faith in God are constantly shown
their own inability to live for Him, apart
from His empowerment.

TIPS AND ENCOURAGEMENT

≡ As you memorize longer verses, do
not be intimidated by the length of
any verse. Begin by reading it over
a few more times in the first day or
two of your memorization. You may
break it down into each sentence and
focus on them singly. In this case,
if you simply read the verse over
and over for a couple of days, then
memorize about nine words a day,
you will easily have it all memorized
in a week.

≡ How much have you learned about God from memorizing His Word? Review past verses to remind yourself how He has led you.

REVIEW

Isaiah 40:31
John 5:24
Psalm 46:1–2
Psalm 9:9–10

WEEK 36

BIBLE MEMORY VERSE

I am crucified with Christ: nevertheless I live;
yet not I, but Christ liveth in me: and the life
which I now live in the flesh I live by the faith
of the Son of God, who loved me,
and gave himself for me.
GALATIANS 2:20 KJV

I have been crucified with Christ and I no longer
live, but Christ lives in me. The life I now live in
the body, I live by faith in the Son of God,
who loved me and gave himself for me.
GALATIANS 2:20 NIV

My old self has been crucified with Christ.
It is no longer I who live, but Christ lives in me.
So I live in this earthly body by trusting in
the Son of God, who loved me and
gave himself for me.
GALATIANS 2:20 NLT

Topic

Salvation

Insight

In saving us, Jesus is not simply making us better but creating totally new people, whose sinful lives have died with Him. God lives in our hearts because of His sacrifice.

Tips and Encouragement

= Some verses powerfully impact us as we read them. We may be encouraged to live for Christ more powerfully or we may feel discouraged, thinking we can never accomplish this. Either way, we need to trust in God's power to work in our lives.

= Has this verse become so commonplace in your life that you fail to respond to it? Think back to the days when you were a very young Christian. What would it have meant to you then? How did your life change?

Review

Colossians 3:1–2
Isaiah 40:31
John 5:24
Psalm 46:1–2
Psalm 9:9–10
Hebrews 4:12

WEEK 37

BIBLE MEMORY VERSE

*Blessed is the man that walketh not in the counsel
of the ungodly, nor standeth in the way of sinners,
nor sitteth in the seat of the scornful.
But his delight is in the law of the LORD;
and in his law doth he meditate day and night.*
PSALM 1:1–2 KJV

*Blessed is the one who does not walk in step with
the wicked or stand in the way that sinners
take or sit in the company of mockers,
but whose delight is in the law of the LORD,
and who meditates on his law day and night.*
PSALM 1:1–2 NIV

*Oh, the joys of those who do not follow the advice
of the wicked, or stand around with sinners,
or join in with mockers. But they delight in the
law of the LORD, meditating on it day and night.*
PSALM 1:1–2 NLT

TOPIC

Seeking God

INSIGHT

Psalm 1 compares the blessed person, or
believer, to the wicked, or unbelieving, one.
Though the world says otherwise, scripture
tells us that trusting in God makes for a joy-
ful life.

TIPS AND ENCOURAGEMENT

≡ Standing up against sin may not always seem blessed, yet we believe in
   God's Word and eventually find that
   it is true. Have you found yourself
   doubting the truth of God's Word,
   only to have it prove itself in your
   eyes?

≡ What encourages you most to memorize God's Word? Is it seeing the way
   it works in your life, the joy you have
   in knowing God more deeply, or the
   impact it has on others when you
   share it? Focus on whatever encourages you to memorize if you just

don't feel like spending time doing it. Make it your goal to share God's truth with others.

Review

Psalm 46:1–2
Psalm 9:9–10
Hebrews 4:12
Galatians 2:20

WEEK 38

BIBLE MEMORY VERSE

Give, and it shall be given unto you;
good measure, pressed down, and shaken together,
and running over, shall men give into your
bosom. For with the same measure that ye mete
withal it shall be measured to you again.
LUKE 6:38 KJV

"Give, and it will be given to you.
A good measure, pressed down, shaken together
and running over, will be poured into your lap.
For with the measure you use, it will be
measured to you."
LUKE 6:38 NIV

"Give, and you will receive. Your gift will return
to you in full — pressed down, shaken together to
make room for more, running over, and poured
into your lap. The amount you give will
determine the amount you get back."
LUKE 6:38 NLT

Topic

Christian Life

Insight

Though Christians often use this verse to encourage monetary giving, in context, it is talking about judging others. Forgive, and you will also be forgiven when you sin.

Tips and Encouragement

= Are you making use of these verses in your own life and attempting to understand them better? Do not allow your memorization to become rote learning, but interact with the verses day by day.

= Are you using these verses to help you understand and help others? The Word of God should be having an impact on your Christian walk, not just on your spiritual understanding of the relationship between yourself and God.

REVIEW

Psalm 9:9–10
Hebrews 4:12
Galatians 2:20
Psalm 1:1–2

WEEK 39

BIBLE MEMORY VERSE

*All scripture is given by inspiration of God,
and is profitable for doctrine, for reproof,
for correction, for instruction in righteousness:
That the man of God may be perfect, thoroughly
furnished unto all good works.*
2 TIMOTHY 3:16–17 KJV

*All Scripture is God-breathed and is useful for
teaching, rebuking, correcting and training in
righteousness, so that the servant of God may be
thoroughly equipped for every good work.*
2 TIMOTHY 3:16–17 NIV

*All Scripture is inspired by God and is useful to
teach us what is true and to make us realize what
is wrong in our lives. It corrects us when we are
wrong and teaches us to do what is right.
God uses it to prepare and equip his people
to do every good work.*
2 TIMOTHY 3:16–17 NLT

Topic

God's Word

Insight

Paul pointed to Timothy's lifelong acquaintance with scripture as the source of this young man's wisdom in spiritual things. Through His Word, God had equipped the young pastor to lead a congregation.

Tips and Encouragement

- It can be spiritually challenging to take the Word at its word. We don't have to be Christians for long before we understand that scripture is both an encouragement and a challenge. Though we may not like God's correction in our lives, it is an important part of our spiritual walks. How we accept it tells a lot about our spiritual maturity. None of us are perfect, but God is perfecting our lives through His Spirit.

- How well equipped are you as a believer? As a leader? How can memorization help you to be better equipped?

- When you have almost finished memorizing a verse, do you go back over the whole verse again, to make sure you have memorized it correctly? It's easy to slip up on memorization when you think you have it down pat.

REVIEW

Hebrews 4:12
Galatians 2:20
Psalm 1:1–2
Luke 6:38

WEEK 40

BIBLE MEMORY VERSE

*Ask, and it shall be given you; seek, and ye shall
find; knock, and it shall be opened unto you:
For every one that asketh receiveth;
and he that seeketh findeth; and to him
that knocketh it shall be opened.*
MATTHEW 7:7–8 KJV

*"Ask and it will be given to you; seek and you will
find; knock and the door will be opened to you.
For everyone who asks receives; the one who seeks
finds; and to the one who knocks,
the door will be opened."*
MATTHEW 7:7–8 NIV

*"Keep on asking, and you will receive what you
ask for. Keep on seeking, and you will find.
Keep on knocking, and the door will be opened
to you. For everyone who asks, receives. Everyone
who seeks, finds. And to everyone who knocks,
the door will be opened."*
MATTHEW 7:7–8 NLT

Topic

Seeking God

Insight

In these verses God isn't promising that every Christian will have an unending succession of luxuries, but that He will give believers the good things they truly need. When we have a real need and seek God persistently, we can count on Him to provide.

Tips and Encouragement

≡ When you memorize a verse, make certain you know what it really means. Otherwise, you may end up sharing the verse but not conveying its real meaning to another person. If necessary, pick up your Bible and read the surrounding verses.

≡ If you share a verse, and another Christian sparks a heated debate with you on its meaning, you may want to spend some time in the scripture and in Bible commentaries to be sure you understand the Word properly.

Too much heated debate without knowledge leads to division, not real understanding.

REVIEW

Galatians 2:20
Psalm 1:1–2
Luke 6:38
2 Timothy 3:16–17

WEEK 41

BIBLE MEMORY VERSE

Be careful for nothing; but in every thing by prayer and supplication with thanksgiving let your requests be made known unto God. And the peace of God, which passeth all understanding, shall keep your hearts and minds through Christ Jesus.
PHILIPPIANS 4:6–7 KJV

Do not be anxious about anything, but in every situation, by prayer and petition, with thanksgiving, present your requests to God. And the peace of God, which transcends all understanding, will guard your hearts and your minds in Christ Jesus.
PHILIPPIANS 4:6–7 NIV

Don't worry about anything; instead, pray about everything. Tell God what you need, and thank him for all he has done. Then you will experience God's peace, which exceeds anything we can understand. His peace will guard your hearts and minds as you live in Christ Jesus.
PHILIPPIANS 4:6–7 NLT

TOPIC

Christian Life

INSIGHT

Paul encouraged the Philippian church, which was facing some opposition, to trust in God and bring all their concerns to Him.

TIPS AND ENCOURAGEMENT

≡ As you memorize these verses, are you also putting them into practice? This is a good verse to make a part of your life. What actions does Paul tell the Philippians to put into practice that can keep them from worrying? What are the results they can expect?

REVIEW

Psalm 1:1–2
Luke 6:38
2 Timothy 3:16–17
Matthew 7:7–8

WEEK 42

BIBLE MEMORY VERSE

*And he said to them all, If any man will come
after me, let him deny himself, and take up his
cross daily, and follow me. For whosoever will
save his life shall lose it: but whosoever will lose
his life for my sake, the same shall save it.*
LUKE 9:23–24 KJV

*Then he said to them all: "Whoever wants to
be my disciple must deny themselves and take
up their cross daily and follow me. For whoever
wants to save their life will lose it, but whoever
loses their life for me will save it."*
LUKE 9:23–24 NIV

*Then he said to the crowd, "If any of you wants
to be my follower, you must turn from your
selfish ways, take up your cross daily,
and follow me. If you try to hang on to your life,
you will lose it. But if you give up your life for
my sake, you will save it."*
LUKE 9:23–24 NLT

TOPIC

Seeking God

INSIGHT

Jesus warns that the Christian life is not a free ride. Just as our salvation cost Him His life, a real faith is costly for us, too. But the benefits of our small sacrifice now have eternal results.

TIPS AND ENCOURAGEMENT

- If you are having trouble remembering the chapter and verses of the texts you've memorized, spend some time connecting the two up in your mind. Focus on the reference before you say the verse, since the last part of your memorization may not easily stick in your mind. Remind yourself that you have not completed your memorization if you cannot tell where the verse is in scripture.

Review

Galatians 2:20
Psalm 1:1–2
Luke 6:38
2 Timothy 3:16–17
Matthew 7:7–8
Philippians 4:6–7

WEEK 43

BIBLE MEMORY VERSE

*Be sober, be vigilant; because your adversary
the devil, as a roaring lion, walketh about,
seeking whom he may devour: Whom resist stedfast
in the faith, knowing that the same afflictions are
accomplished in your brethren that are
in the world.*
1 PETER 5:8–9 KJV

*Be alert and of sober mind. Your enemy the devil
prowls around like a roaring lion looking for
someone to devour. Resist him, standing firm
in the faith, because you know that the family of
believers throughout the world is undergoing
the same kind of sufferings.*
1 PETER 5:8–9 NIV

*Stay alert! Watch out for your great enemy,
the devil. He prowls around like a roaring lion,
looking for someone to devour. Stand firm
against him, and be strong in your faith.
Remember that your Christian brothers and
sisters all over the world are going through
the same kind of suffering you are.*
1 PETER 5:8–9 NLT

TOPIC

Christian Life

INSIGHT

Though the Christian life brings joy, it also has a serious side. The accuser, Satan, lies in wait to tempt frivolous believers. Peter calls God's people to be earnest in their belief and stand against opposition.

TIPS AND ENCOURAGEMENT

- No matter what trial you face, God knows about it. When God commands you to stand firm, He also provides you with the strength to do it, as you trust in Him. This applies to Bible memorization, too!

- Knowing you will face opposition, prepare for it by studying and memorizing God's Word. It will strengthen and encourage you and help you to respond to those who attack your faith. The more verses you have under your belt, the better prepared you will be.

Review

2 Timothy 3:16–17
Matthew 7:7–8
Philippians 4:6–7
Luke 9:23–24

WEEK 44

BIBLE MEMORY VERSE

That if thou shalt confess with thy mouth the Lord Jesus, and shalt believe in thine heart that God hath raised him from the dead, thou shalt be saved. For with the heart man believeth unto righteousness; and with the mouth confession is made unto salvation.
ROMANS 10:9–10 KJV

If you declare with your mouth, "Jesus is Lord," and believe in your heart that God raised him from the dead, you will be saved. For it is with your heart that you believe and are justified, and it is with your mouth that you profess your faith and are saved.
ROMANS 10:9–10 NIV

If you confess with your mouth that Jesus is Lord and believe in your heart that God raised him from the dead, you will be saved. For it is by believing in your heart that you are made right with God, and it is by confessing with your mouth that you are saved.
ROMANS 10:9–10 NLT

Topic

Salvation

Insight

God calls on Christians to share their faith so that all may hear of His gracious love. To be a Christian, one cannot believe in anyone but Christ. Being a Christian also takes a serious commitment and trust in Him alone.

Tips and Encouragement

- Many people balk at this scriptural truth because they'd like to go with the flow and believe that heaven has no limitations. But this verse points out the critical part of belief in Christ: the truth that He is the only way to God. It is an important truth to be able to share with others.

- Do you avoid memorizing verses that are uncomfortable? Memorizing the "happy" verses of scripture may be encouraging to you and others, but if you do only that, you are avoiding the whole counsel of God. Don't miss

out on all God wants you to know
about Him and His salvation.

Review

Matthew 7:7–8
Philippians 4:6–7
Luke 9:23–24
1 Peter 5:8–9

WEEK 45

The LORD is my rock, and my fortress, and my deliverer; my God, my strength, in whom I will trust; my buckler, and the horn of my salvation, and my high tower. I will call upon the LORD, who is worthy to be praised: so shall I be saved from mine enemies.
PSALM 18:2–3 KJV

The LORD is my rock, my fortress and my deliverer; my God is my rock, in whom I take refuge, my shield and the horn of my salvation, my stronghold. I called to the LORD, who is worthy of praise, and I have been saved from my enemies.
PSALM 18:2–3 NIV

The LORD is my rock, my fortress, and my savior; my God is my rock, in whom I find protection. He is my shield, the power that saves me, and my place of safety. I called on the LORD, who is worthy of praise, and he saved me from my enemies.
PSALM 18:2–3 NLT

Topic

Our God

Insight

David penned these words after God had rescued him from his enemies, including King Saul, who sought his life. If David could trust the Lord in such circumstances, how much more can we trust Him?

Tips and Encouragement

≡ Petra's song "I Will Call upon the Lord" may help you with verse 3, if you use the King James Version of the Bible for your memorization. If this tune is already in your head, you have the verse memorized!

≡ When you have memorized verse 3, you have also memorized 2 Samuel 22:4, since it is repeated there.

REVIEW

Philippians 4:6–7
Luke 9:23–24
1 Peter 5:8–9
Romans 10:9–10

WEEK 46

BIBLE MEMORY VERSE

Surely he hath borne our griefs, and carried our sorrows: yet we did esteem him stricken, smitten of God, and afflicted. But he was wounded for our transgressions, he was bruised for our iniquities: the chastisement of our peace was upon him; and with his stripes we are healed.
ISAIAH 53:4–5 KJV

Surely he took up our pain and bore our suffering, yet we considered him punished by God, stricken by him, and afflicted. But he was pierced for our transgressions, he was crushed for our iniquities; the punishment that brought us peace was on him, and by his wounds we are healed.
ISAIAH 53:4–5 NIV

Yet it was our weaknesses he carried; it was our sorrows that weighed him down. And we thought his troubles were a punishment from God, a punishment for his own sins! But he was pierced for our rebellion, crushed for our sins. He was beaten so we could be whole. He was whipped so we could be healed.
ISAIAH 53:4–5 NLT

TOPIC

Salvation

INSIGHT

Centuries before Jesus was born, the prophet Isaiah spoke these words of Jesus, the Suffering Servant, who would die for our sins.

TIPS AND ENCOURAGEMENT

≡   Rather than giving up on a memorization passage because it seems "too long," break it up into two weeks of memorization. Better to keep up with a consistent pattern than to give up on your memorization plan. But you may also find that doing the whole passage is easier than you think. Read over the whole passage as you start your memorization, then begin memorizing as usual. You may find you have completed the whole passage by the end of the week.

≡ If you are a fan of Handel's oratorio *Messiah*, these words may be familiar to you. Let that help you along with your memorization.

Review

Luke 9:23–24
1 Peter 5:8–9
Romans 10:9–10
Psalm 18:2–3

WEEK 47

BIBLE MEMORY VERSE

And thou shalt love the Lord thy God with all thy heart, and with all thy soul, and with all thy mind, and with all thy strength: this is the first commandment. And the second is like, namely this, Thou shalt love thy neighbour as thyself. There is none other commandment greater than these.
MARK 12:30–31 KJV

"'Love the Lord your God with all your heart and with all your soul and with all your mind and with all your strength.' The second is this: 'Love your neighbor as yourself.' There is no commandment greater than these."
MARK 12:30–31 NIV

"'And you must love the LORD your God with all your heart, all your soul, all your mind, and all your strength.' The second is equally important: 'Love your neighbor as yourself.' No other commandment is greater than these."
MARK 12:30–31 NLT

TOPIC

Christian Life

INSIGHT

Jewish law included many commandments
on how to please God, from rituals to guide-
lines for personal piety. When a scribe asked
Jesus which one was the most important, this
was His response.

TIPS AND ENCOURAGEMENT

= The focus of your memorization
should be improving your walk
with the Lord by coming to know
His commandments. But knowing
the words alone will be an empty
effort if your relationship with God
isn't warm and deep. How can this
verse help you reach that goal?

REVIEW

1 Peter 5:8–9
Romans 10:9–10
Psalm 18:2–3
Isaiah 53:4–5

WEEK 48

BIBLE MEMORY VERSE

*Go ye therefore, and teach all nations, baptizing
them in the name of the Father, and of the Son,
and of the Holy Ghost: Teaching them to observe
all things whatsoever I have commanded you:
and, lo, I am with you always, even unto
the end of the world. Amen.*
MATTHEW 28:19–20 KJV

*"Therefore go and make disciples of all nations,
baptizing them in the name of the Father and of
the Son and of the Holy Spirit, and teaching them
to obey everything I have commanded you.
And surely I am with you always,
to the very end of the age."*
MATTHEW 28:19–20 NIV

*"Therefore, go and make disciples of all the
nations, baptizing them in the name of the Father
and the Son and the Holy Spirit. Teach these new
disciples to obey all the commands I have given
you. And be sure of this: I am with you always,
even to the end of the age."*
MATTHEW 28:19–20 NLT

TOPIC

Faith

INSIGHT

Known as the Great Commission, these verses, spoken by Jesus, have inspired Christians throughout the ages to spread the Good News of Jesus.

TIPS AND ENCOURAGEMENT

- God not only encourages us and tells us about Himself through scripture, He also commands us to take action concerning our beliefs. How is this a challenge to you? An encouragement?

REVIEW

Luke 9:23–24
1 Peter 5:8–9
Romans 10:9–10
Psalm 18:2–3
Isaiah 53:4–5
Mark 12:30–31

WEEK 49

BIBLE MEMORY VERSE

*Therefore I say unto you, Take no thought for
your life, what ye shall eat, or what ye shall
drink; nor yet for your body, what ye shall put
on. Is not the life more than meat, and the body
than raiment? Behold the fowls of the air:
for they sow not, neither do they reap,
nor gather into barns; yet your heavenly Father
feedeth them. Are ye not much better than they?*
MATTHEW 6:25–26 KJV

*"Therefore I tell you, do not worry about your life,
what you will eat or drink; or about your body,
what you will wear. Is not life more than food,
and the body more than clothes? Look at the birds
of the air; they do not sow or reap or store away in
barns, and yet your heavenly Father feeds them.
Are you not much more valuable than they?"*
MATTHEW 6:25–26 NIV

"That is why I tell you not to worry about everyday life — whether you have enough food and drink, or enough clothes to wear. Isn't life more than food, and your body more than clothing? Look at the birds. They don't plant or harvest or store food in barns, for your heavenly Father feeds them. And aren't you far more valuable to him than they are?"

MATTHEW 6:25–26 NLT

TOPIC

Seeking God

INSIGHT

This comforting passage turns Christians away from concern about daily needs and toward trust of God. He knows our every need, and we can seek His kingdom without worrying that He will fail us.

TIPS AND ENCOURAGEMENT

≡ Begin to think about verses you'd like to memorize when you finish the *Bible Memory Plan*. You may begin with those in More Verses to Memorize, at the end of the book, but you will also need to create a plan that helps you memorize for the rest of your life. If you have a favorite devotional, such as *My Utmost for His Highest*, perhaps you will want to use the daily verses as fuel for your memorization. If your Bible study recommends verses, you may want to use them.

≡ To create a memorization plan, you could also copy down verses as you read your Bible or use other materials to study the Word. Write them on file cards and place them in a file card box, available at any stationery store, then use them as you need them. Just make certain you do not repeat the verses you already have memorized!

REVIEW

Psalm 18:2–3
Isaiah 53:4–5
Mark 12:30–31
Matthew 28:19–20

WEEK 50

BIBLE MEMORY VERSE

*For God so loved the world, that he gave his only
begotten Son, that whosoever believeth in him
should not perish, but have everlasting life.
For God sent not his Son into the world to condemn
the world; but that the world through him might
be saved. He that believeth on him is not
condemned: but he that believeth not is
condemned already, because he hath not believed
in the name of the only begotten Son of God.*
JOHN 3:16–18 KJV

*"For God so loved the world that he gave his
one and only Son, that whoever believes in him
shall not perish but have eternal life. For God
did not send his Son into the world to condemn
the world, but to save the world through him.
Whoever believes in him is not condemned,
but whoever does not believe stands condemned
already because they have not believed in the
name of God's one and only Son."*
JOHN 3:16–18 NIV

*"For God loved the world so much that he gave
his one and only Son, so that everyone who
believes in him will not perish but have eternal life.
God sent his Son into the world not to judge the
world, but to save the world through him.
There is no judgment against anyone who
believes in him. But anyone who does not believe
in him has already been judged for not believing
in God's one and only Son."*
JOHN 3:16–18 NLT

TOPIC

Salvation

INSIGHT

John 3:16 is probably the most familiar Bible
verse. But how many people have memorized the verses that follow? By memorizing
them, we complete our picture of the salvation God offers to those who will believe.

TIPS AND ENCOURAGEMENT

- Don't shrug off memorizing familiar verses because you feel you know them too well and it would be too easy. Instead, place them in context by memorizing some verses around them, too. You'll have a challenge and will be able to make effective use of the verse you already know.

REVIEW

Isaiah 53:4–5
Mark 12:30–31
Matthew 28:19–20
Matthew 6:25–26

WEEK 51

BIBLE MEMORY VERSE

*But now the righteousness of God without the
law is manifested, being witnessed by the law
and the prophets; even the righteousness of God
which is by faith of Jesus Christ unto all and
upon all them that believe: for there is no
difference: For all have sinned, and come short of
the glory of God; being justified freely by his grace
through the redemption that is in Christ Jesus.*
ROMANS 3:21–24 KJV

*But now apart from the law the righteousness of
God has been made known, to which the Law and
the Prophets testify. This righteousness is given
through faith in Jesus Christ to all who believe.
There is no difference between Jew and Gentile,
for all have sinned and fall short of the glory of
God, and are justified freely by his grace through
the redemption that came by Christ Jesus.*
ROMANS 3:21–24 NIV

But now God has shown us a way to be made
right with him without keeping the requirements
of the law, as was promised in the writings of
Moses and the prophets long ago. We are made
right with God by placing our faith in Jesus
Christ. And this is true for everyone who believes,
no matter who we are. For everyone has sinned;
we all fall short of God's glorious standard.
Yet God, with undeserved kindness, declares that
we are righteous. He did this through Christ Jesus
when he freed us from the penalty for our sins.
ROMANS 3:21–24 NLT

TOPIC

Salvation

INSIGHT

Nothing we can do will make us good
enough to approach our holy God. The apostle Paul knew this from personal experience,
since he had been a zealous Jew, rigorous in
his observance of the Law. Only faith in Jesus
justifies us with the Lord.

Tips and Encouragement

- When you choose verses to memorize on your own, pick some that are shorter and some that are longer. That way you will be able to keep up with your memorization plan even when your life is busy.

- Choose verses on different topics, so that you get a good command of God's Word. Though you may want to memorize one topic for an extended period of time, be certain you don't become stuck in one area, or you'll be a one-sided Christian in your Bible memorization.

- As you've moved through the book, the verses you've memorized have gotten longer. Has memorization become easier, or have you simply figured out the best way to memorize? Either way, congratulations on your accomplishment.

Review

Mark 12:30–31
Matthew 28:19–20
Matthew 6:25–26
John 3:16–18

WEEK 52

BIBLE MEMORY VERSE

*Wherefore seeing we also are compassed about
with so great a cloud of witnesses, let us lay aside
every weight, and the sin which doth so easily
beset us, and let us run with patience the race
that is set before us, looking unto Jesus the author
and finisher of our faith; who for the joy that was
set before him endured the cross, despising
the shame, and is set down at the right hand
of the throne of God.*
HEBREWS 12:1–2 KJV

*Therefore, since we are surrounded by such a
great cloud of witnesses, let us throw off
everything that hinders and the sin that so easily
entangles. And let us run with perseverance the
race marked out for us, fixing our eyes on Jesus,
the pioneer and perfecter of faith.
For the joy set before him he endured the cross,
scorning its shame, and sat down at the right
hand of the throne of God.*
HEBREWS 12:1–2 NIV

*Therefore, since we are surrounded by such a
huge crowd of witnesses to the life of faith,
let us strip off every weight that slows us down,
especially the sin that so easily trips us up.
And let us run with endurance the race God has
set before us. We do this by keeping our eyes on
Jesus, the champion who initiates and perfects our
faith. Because of the joy awaiting him, he endured
the cross, disregarding its shame. Now he is seated
in the place of honor beside God's throne.*

HEBREWS 12:1–2 NLT

TOPIC

Our God

INSIGHT

We do not run the faith race alone: Others
have gone before us and have successfully
completed the course. We can look to them
for inspiration when the course becomes
hard and our breathing labored. If we keep
Jesus in our minds and hearts as we run,
we will be victorious.